First published in North America
by Annick Press 2002
Text © 2001 Meg Clibbon
Illustrations © 2001 Lucy Clibbon
Originally published by Zero To Ten Limited
(a member of the Evans Publishing Group)
© Zero To Ten Limited 2001

Cataloging in Publication Data
Clibbon, Meg
Imagine you're a fairy
North American edition
(Imagine this! series)
ISBN 1-55037-743-4 (bound).--ISBN 1-55037-742-6 (pbk.)

1. Fairies--Juvenile literature. I. Clibbon, Lucy II.Title.
III. Clibbon, Meg. Imagine this! series.

CUR

GR549.C55 2002   j398'.45   C2002-900424-1

Distributed in Canada and the U.S.A. by Firefly Books Ltd.

www.annickpress.com

Printed in Hong Kong.

Imagine you're a Fairy!

Magic Meg
(also known as Meg Clibbon)

used to live in the Enchanted Forest where she taught fledgling fairies, pixies, and elves to read runes and write the magic alphabet. The most important lessons she taught were how to fly on moonbeams and gossamer into the land of dreams.

Lucy Loveheart
(also known as Lucy Clibbon)

has a special interest in fairies. She is particularly fascinated by the Enchanted Forest and spends much of her time daydreaming about it. She works mainly in watercolor, collage, stickers, and glitter, but she also uses a little bit of magic and fairy dust.

We would like to dedicate this book to three wonderful fairy godmothers:

Joan, Connie, and Mary.

What is a fairy?

*It is very difficult to describe
fairies because they are made out of
the imagination, not out of words.
Human beings very rarely meet fairies,
but those who have say that:
Fairies are usually smaller than humans.
Fairies are very secret.
Fairies live in an enchanted world.
Fairies do magic.*

What do fairies look like?

There are lots of different kinds of fairies.

They come in many different shapes and sizes.

Tiara

Regal expression

Good luck charm

Magic wand

Straight back

Wings

Stars and fairy dust

Flying shoes

Whatever they look like, all fairies are very clever and very magical.

Different types of fairies

Brownies: very kindly

Pixies: very fast and lively

Goblins: ugly little demons, but clever

Sprites: almost invisible

Gnomes: live underground

Not all fairies are pretty, with gauzy rainbow wings and frilly frocks. Some are rough and tough and very naughty. Some are spiteful and many of them are ugly and have no kind of dress sense. Here are some of the other types.

Imps: very naughty

Elves: mischievous, but good leaders

Tooth fairies: like living near humans

The Boogeyman: bad-tempered

Banshees: female and scream a lot

Leprechauns

They live in Ireland and look like very small old men. They like drinking a drink called poteen, which makes them rather spiteful. They guard treasure buried in pots and hide it at the end of rainbows. They carry two purses, one with a magic coin and one with fool's gold.

Jack-muh-lantern
These mysterious lights live in swamps and marshes and lure humans into them with their elf-fire.

The little people
They live in the Isle of Man (United Kingdom), where people still believe in fairies. They wear red caps and green jackets and hunt with multicolored hounds.

Where do fairies live?

Nobody is quite sure where fairies live. They could live in dark, creepy caves or pretty little cottages or under delicate, dusky toadstools, or in silvery cobweb nets swinging in the branches of trees ... but nobody really knows. They appear magically at the most unexpected moments and then they disappear again.

Where do they come from?
Where do they go to?
Where do you think
they live?

Outfits and clothes

Fairies need special outfits for special occasions.

Disguise

Casual outfit

Magic-making outfit

Party outfit

Equipment and accessories

Fairies need special accessories to help them with their work.

Magic wands

Handbag

Flying shoes

Cloak of invisibility

Book of spells

Magic potion

Fairy dust

Flower-fairy pollen

Nectar of toadstools

Wings

Tiaras

Glitter

Magic and spells

*Fairies can do lots of magical things,
like flying, appearing and disappearing,
and making dreams come true. In order to
do magic it is essential to have a wand,
some wings, some fairy dust, a tiara
(or a baseball cap will do), and a book of spells.
A fairy's book of spells is very special
and very secret, but here are some examples
of typical fairy spells.*

Secret spell #115

Magic spell for good luck

You will need:

1 cup of daisy heads

2 spoonfuls of rosebuds

8 spoonfuls of morning dew

1 four-leaved clover
(a three-leaved clover will sometimes
work if you can't find one)

1 magic wand

1 mixing bowl

Directions

1. Mix the daisy heads, rosebuds,
and morning dew in mixing bowl.

2. Place bowl by your feet.

3. Hold clover in your right hand.

4. Hold wand upright in left hand.

5. Close eyes and say,
"Make my dream come true!"

Things that go wrong

Magic is a tricky thing and inexperienced fairies often get it wrong. It has been known for fairies to crash-land in bramble bushes because they have not taken enough care of their wings. Fairy dust has a nasty habit of making you sneeze. It is very awkward to appear magically in the wrong place at the wrong time. Even worse is when a magic spell makes a nightmare come true instead of a lovely dream. Not all fairies are good. Some are rather bad and they make things go wrong on purpose.

Secret spell #409

Magic spell for general mischief

You will need:
1 cup of water
3 old chestnuts (or acorns)
1 handful of playground dust
2 pieces of adhesive tape
1 spoonful of earth
4 old oak leaves

Directions
Place all the ingredients into an old tin in the dead of night (around 9 o'clock). Use wand in position A (see page about Wand Practice). Shout, "Banshee! Banshee!" and spell will be effective.

Wand practice

Hold wand firmly in hand. Smooth action.
Concentration essential.

Polish wand after use.
Keep in a safe place.

A. Making magic spells

B. Turning frogs into princes

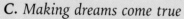

D. Blowing fairy dust everywhere

C. Making dreams come true

Flying practice

For best results do
flying practice unobserved.
Avoid built-up areas.
Always aim for
smooth landing.

A. *The flutter position*

B. *Swooping upwards*

Polish wings with fairy dust after use.
Hang up in fairy closet.

C. *Butterfly flying*

D. *Gliding*

Fairy godmothers

These are special fairies because they come in human form. A fairy godmother can be young or middle-aged, but the favorite sort of fairy godmother is quite old, with a wrinkly face and a lovely, encouraging smile.

Fairy godmothers are invited to lots of their godchildren's birthday parties. The children's parents expect special presents such as health, kindness, bravery, patience, cheerfulness, obedience, and good fortune … but the children would rather have toys or chocolate.

At the moment there are not many fairy godfathers, but this is considered to be very unfair and the Fairy Union (F.U.N.) is looking into it because there is a great demand for good fairy godfathers.

The Fairy Union (F.U.N.)

The Fairy Union (F.U.N.) insists that all fairies follow a strict code of conduct and obey the rules for fairies.

Rules

1. Always carry your wand, although it may be disguised as something else under certain circumstances.
2. Always be on the lookout for wicked witches who may cast horrid spells.
3. Look after your wings properly. Hang them up before you go to bed at night and polish them with fairy dust once a week.
4. Never stick out your tongue at a fairy godmother or the fairy king or you may get turned into a pumpkin.

Motto: Imagine magic and make-believe.

The Enchanted Forest

1. Gossamer clouds – dreams come true when you sleep in these.

2. Tooth-fairy factory – tooth fairies collect children's baby teeth when they fall out and grind them down very finely to use in fairy dust.

3. Stars – used in dreams and for making glitter.

4. Flying school – all young fairies must attend.

5. Store cupboard – safe storage for magic dust.

6. Wing polishers – a specially trained team of elves to polish fairies' wings.

7. Boutique – where fairies buy designer outfits.

8. Wand shop – for new wands and repairs.

9. Fairy ring – the fairies' dancing ground.

10. Wishing well – the water from this well is used in magic potions.

11. Toadstools – where fairies sit to think or have their homes.

12. Cobweb cradles – baby fairies never cry when they are rocked in these.

13. Garden – where the fairies grow vegetables.

Jobs list

1. Wand practice.

2. Prepare potions
to take to sick creatures in the
Enchanted forest.

3. Water flowers and herbs
in the garden.

4. Make new magic spells
and practice old ones.

5. Polish wings, wand,
and flying shoes.

6. Contact members of F.U.N.
and invite to Moonlight Ball.

7. Make Magic Fairy Bars for afternoon snack.

Fairy words

gossamer

pumpkin

ward

disappear

magic

moon beam

invisible

toadstool

cobwebs

shimmer

secrets

mischief

potion

tiara

glitter

disguise

flutter

sprinkle

rosebud

abracadabra

How many new words can you make from the letters in
Enchanted Forest?

Famous fairies

Tinkerbell

Tinkerbell is a pretty little fairy who lives in Never Never land. This is in the story Peter Pan by J.M. Barrie. She has great fun with Peter Pan and the Lost Boys, until a girl called Wendy comes to live there too. Tinkerbell is so jealous that she causes a great deal of mischief and nearly loses her magical powers before everything turns out well in the end.

Titania, Oberon, and Puck

These are famous fairies in a play called A Midsummer Night's Dream by William Shakespeare. Titania is the very beautiful Queen of the Fairies and Oberon is the powerful King of the Fairies. All through the play they weave magic spells with the help of their cunning little fairy servant, called Puck, who makes life very difficult for a lot of people. This story turns out well in the end too. Thank goodness.

Famous fairy godmothers

The most famous fairy
godmothers appear in the stories
Cinderella and The Sleeping Beauty.
In both stories the beautiful heroines need
a lot of help from their fairy godmothers.
Cinderella needs a coach, a new pair of glass
slippers, a handsome prince, a designer ball gown,
and goodness knows what else. She is saved from
a life of housework by her very kind godmother.

The Sleeping Beauty is imprisoned inside a rose
bush and would still be there if her fairy
godmother had not arranged for a passing
prince to cut her out and wake her up
with a kiss. This must have been
rather a shock for her.

Things to do

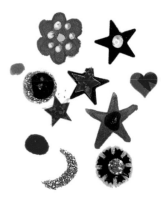

Fairy dust

Fairy dust helps to make magic properly.
Make your own fairy dust by mixing together:
1 pinch of silver glitter
1 pinch of gold glitter
1 pinch of small sequins
Put together in a little bottle marked "Fairy Dust."
Use sparingly and sprinkle wherever
and whenever needed.

Make a crown

Cut a strip of silver paper big enough to
wrap around your head. Glue the ends together
and decorate with magic shapes of your choice.

Make a wand

Wands make things appear and disappear and
are very good for helping spells. To make your
own, cut out a large star shape
and decorate with glitter, stars, and hearts.
Attach this to a long stick painted in
the color of your choice.

Fairy bars

You will need:
75g (2½ oz.) margarine or butter
75g (2½ oz.) breakfast cereal (cornflakes or puffed rice)
1 tablespoon syrup
2 chocolate bars
Fresh flowers to decorate

Directions

Place margarine or butter into saucepan. Add chocolate bars and syrup. Melt on low heat. Turn off heat and stir cereal in until coated. Put onto greased tray and when almost cool cut into bars. Arrange bars on pretty plate and decorate with flower petals. (Watch them disappear like magic!)

Practice flying

You'll need wings first. Make your wings by cutting out a piece of net or shimmery material into wing shapes. Ask your fairy godmother to help you. Then decorate with star and heart shapes and glitter. Only a few very special fairies can really fly, but if you run or skip around the yard and flap your arms up and down with wings attached, it almost feels like flying.